My Life and My Songs

My Life and My Songs

A Book of English Poems

BIBHAKAR DUTTA

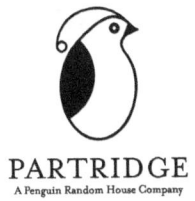

PARTRIDGE
A Penguin Random House Company

To order additional copies of this book, contact
Partridge India
000 800 10062 62
orders.india@partridgepublishing.com

www.partridgepublishing.com/india

CONTENTS

Dedication

This book is solely dedicated to the loving memories of the departed souls of my grandfathers and grandmothers.

A THOUGHTLESS MAN

He never tames his emotion,
his mind is full of jubilance,
he never allows to subjugate himself into temptation;
he is brilliant and a thoughtless man.

He is still searching his lost love,
a huge delusion has wagged his heart,
yet he looks glad.
His soul is broad, but he is a thoughtless man.

He often sits under a shade
and tries to gaze
at the rock standing right before his eyes which has no age.
He never complains of his stress as he is a thoughtless man.

He goes to seaside and observes the ships
coming out of horizon line.
Thus, he is waiting for his love, and hope is the time
for this thoughtless man.

Wind turns its way from spring to summer,
but his love remains still.
He is a thoughtless man,
love rules his life and he has devoted everything.

AMAZING ESSENCE

I miss you,
and the missing is intolerable
my love is my faith,
and you stay in my breath.

This heart just waits,
and forever wants to place
your fantastic, charming percept
by my inmost depth of sense.

Yes, you exist in my deepest sense;
The Love and my respect,
being greatly intense,
are spreading through your amazing essence.

AMAZING!!

I just opened the door,
and sensed the dank morning;
Oh, how hazy the earth is!
my eyes are missing the street.

The park is silent-
that seems, it's still asleep;
this is an hour to refresh
your affection and prolong the friendship.

The parky wind, which brings a message
for the day, is touching my hands,
and my heart being free from trashes, gets so excited.
Oh, how amazing the morning is!! . . .

AN INJURED MIND

An injured mind always cries.
There is no surprise
to calm its eyes.
It never becomes consoled.

An injured mind comes closer to you.
It seeks some advice.
It needs a touch to appease
and to blur its grief.

An injured mind wants to mitigate
its inner grievance,
but someone should approach to make
its soul perfect.

An injured mind can revive.
Just soak out its sadness.
Make it pure
as you're.

BIBHAKAR DUTTA

AN UNDIVIDED SOUL

You and me an undivided soul,
one dedicates but the other is goal.
One can't stand if another steps alone,
we are an undivided soul.

We are entire, we are assimilated
fulfilling one another's wish by intercession;
intelligible is our sense,
and that affection becoming very intense.

You see, we are an undivided soul,
one stays in another's intellect
with a string to intensify love and much to expect.
Yes, we are one—we are perfect.

AS YOU CAME

As you came,
My tune still sings
The songs of love;
Remembering your sweet smile
Past has become
Brilliant to compose love-staff.

As you came,
My heart was going to inflame
By the touch of unclaimed love.
Though the time was too short,
But I still feel it-its sense can't be stopped,
And I never try to declaim again and again!

As you came,
My heart has become perfect
To detect openness
And to find the true intellect.
I deserve my love remain
Ingenuous and plain.

ATTACHMENT

Life lives in crisis,
fantasy is needed everywhere,
this life seeks a synopsis;
and there is only a hope holds the future.

Your philosophy, my previsions,
all depends merely in an anticipation;
but our love grips the perception
which is an ultimate and a perfect destination.

So, I want to explore thoughts with my attachment,
I don't know, how much can I gather the sagaciousness (alone)?
but I do know about the inclination
that regress me towards you.
There is no attainment without you, my love,
You are enough,
yes, my beloved!!

BARE HANDS

Bare hands can't,
but just write loving words for you.
Bare hands can't,
but just write few fair and frank lines for pleasantness and beauty.
My God says, "Wait till the last day of faith,
But be strong and straight
when human wisdom will be fully wrecked".
If you are blessed,
Devote himself to destroy the wicked
lands full of delinquents.
Behold—the Truth is waiting for your sacrifice.
If you want to become His friend
Then proceed,
please don't wait.
Please don't hesitate-
You will be someday great.
Let's raise our hands against Darkness and Disgrace.

BELOVED

You are a grumpy mind,.
love doesn't exist in you,
and without love we are just a shapeless soul,
inaccurate to find
the actual sooth.

You can't deny your passion
which is permanent,
and holds everyone's perception.
This perception decontaminates
our desires, but the highest fruition is love!

But, today, where is the love?
ruthless hearts and frauds
having meaningless longings,
destroy a beneficent heart.
Where is the love?

But, don't worry my beloved,
I still encore my heart
to recall our past-
The past was fruitful
that exchanged our indefinable thrust.

BOUND TO FEEL YOUR LOVE

Bound to feel your love,
Sadness—so painful is my love!
But I'm just bound to feel your love.
Will it be ever dark?
Will you not spark?
So hard, so blurred
But bound to feel your love-
So tough to bear,
So shrill; and I have fear.
Oh dear!
Why don't you care?
Make it clear,
Are you true or a liar?
(Like a night mare)
Do release, please-
It's not really mean
You desire.
Why don't you admire?
No blame, no claim
My love is still glaring
And waiting . . . .
to me you alike,
like a huge tide
knocks my heart-
Just say dear, you are That.
Please make a remark
As I'm bound to feel your love.

BIBHAKAR DUTTA

CARELESS

I stood and sometimes
I was walking by the road side.
I was seeing the passing of cars
I was enjoying the day sometimes.
the day was bright,
and the afternoon's breeze was very sweet.
The heads of the trees were sparkling by day light
standing beside road side.
I was continuing my journey,
and approaching towards my destiny slowly.
Then I was a thoughtless.
I was a careless,
but I was not a feeling-less (then).
The past, reminding me of those Green days,
was shaking my careless mind.
My mind stippled my sense
recalling those beautiful past days.
Every time I was starting my steps,
you had compressed my thoughts and strength.
Oh my beloved!
I always want you to be with me
and we should bind forever ourselves.
But, I am still a careless.

COLORS

Each good human-character,
that my world bears,
has their own thoughts.
Each person comments
different values about morality.
We all need to control our integrity.
Sometimes you suggest me,
and I also make the evaluations.
It's all about our colorful perceptions.
Someone just spent a dignified life
by writing some meaningful poetry.
Some of them tried to gain over their personal grief
by writing in every page filling the essence emotion.
But few of them
wanted to fight against the system
that had held the worst impression
to us and of course, for the mankind.
After all, the poets are always kind.
They love to add colors
in our mind.
So, my poets are the artist,
and their each poem is an image
filled with excellent colors.

DEEPNESS

Why? . . .
Why??
You always ask me.
You will never be the same
When love will claim
And make you confused again.
To suffer, to pain,
To murmur and to refrain-
They are nothing
But to confuse you again.
Feel the love, and feel the pain.
Again and again . . . .
When love whisper,
You can't refuse,
You can't sustain.
Just recall your beloved
And feel the essence of love.
Yes, love
And only love . . .
Just recall your beloved.
Everything would be worthless
If your love fails to confer Deepness.
Yes, the Deepness . . .

DISCRIMINATION

We, the human beings are blessed with pride
And power.
We have everything as the nature
Helps us giving delicious fruits and flower.

We make our destiny.
We arrange our suitable cultures
Because we are the social being.
God orders us to maintain this stricture.

So, please my friends;
We should not try to overpower
This system making a false pride, power
And discrimination because we all are equal.

We should follow our inner sense.
We all are friends.
This friendship should stay forever, and we will enjoy the
divine recreation.
Hope this world would be free from any social
discrimination.

BIBHAKAR DUTTA

DON'T SAY GOOD BYE

No! no!
Please don't say good bye.
Please . . .
I may come
sailing thousands of mile
to meet you second time.

Please don't say bye,
I may come
removing all—the barriers
and only for your love;
I shall again knock the door.
Yes, I may come.

Please don't say good bye.
Whatever makes me sick,
I don't care.
I shall cross
world's highest crest
for my love's shake.
Please don't say good bye.

ESSENCE

Past, present or the next
but love still exists,
though you stay sometimes in silence,
but you have an essence.

You have a hut
in everyone's heart.
being an intimate pal of hope,
I know, your presence is felt
by your sweet semblance.

Oh love! you do stay,
and occur our sense;
all day we want to feel the essence,
and that I always pray.

BIBHAKAR DUTTA

FAME

The road is now clear
for your love waiting to be united-
just look at her face.
The road is unfaded and excited
being a part of your journey.
The day is also very bright
so you can easily recognize
her face glittering in the light.
I Just pray to my God,
that she would be the same
when she first time came,
and gave me the fame.
I have no claim-
hope she would be the same.

GIFT

That time was a gift,
being dignified,
me and my love used to be prominent
and endearing was the fate.

Love and time, they both exist at same thread,
and to conduct my destiny
was a blissful, heavenly
and perfect to entrust our love.

Still ruling my heart,
the connection may stay evermore;
just hope, the glory would glorify incessantly.
Let's be the one but not a part,
oneness should rule our love.

HE IS GREAT

He is great.
He is a generous by his inbred endowment.
His words are impressive and still glow our pathetic sensation(s).
Each of lines and verse are deathless-
his talent can rake up an exhausted soul.
It can remove the indigence,
and inflame your sense again.
His love, his affection, and his passion
are worthy and a message for next generation.
He was a moderate,
and he could easily sustain
to gain over his life's pain(s).
At last, I must say about his devotion
that enlarges his memory.
He has got all my esteem.
Keats, you are still amazing . . . .

(This poem is dedicated to Late John Keats)

HOPE

Each day ends with hope.
The next day comes with a new hope.
It doesn't matter, how much will you obtain?
But hope always relieves our pain.

It doesn't matter, how much you have suffered?
But the hope has been a friend of your painful heart.
Hope is a friend made with divine essence,
never makes us exaggerative; but saves our soul of being a desert.

So, HOPE, You do exist in our soul, in our heart
and, of course, in our luck.
Bad times already have punished me-
but You always rescue my life against the Dark.

BIBHAKAR DUTTA

HOPE (PART-2)

I have sentiments,
I am careful before
to make any statement.
everyday a new hope
is come out, and that starts the day;
but all wishes are not pure,
God fixes those we deeply pray.
Sometimes a hope,
that slops to bind up our detachments,
doesn't want to flop.
Oh, how amazing you are!
Everyday we have a new hope,
God guides us how to attach
our destinations through a hope.

HOPE DOES EXIST

Hope leaves
and my vehement desires go in vain-
love has left this life
gifting so much pain.

Indolent life of meaningless passion,
bestowing vague promises
decreases the impression
and the world of admonition.

In that mid day, a strong man came;
He had a smiling face and said, 'Oh, my little son
those days were clumsy-
hope does exist, and now it's your turn.'

I thought a lot-
is he the owner who owns the heaven, and rules the hell?
Well, I have stayed in both;
and now, it's time to follow his glory
He wants something,
and I am ready to sacrifice and sustain.

BIBHAKAR DUTTA

I AM FREE

We made a joyous moment
and, it was our last visit.
'You left because I escaped',
you said.
But it's not the Real.
I left because you escaped from my heart
Leaving an agreement.
I will enjoy myself
as I am now free—
But do not look at me
with your jealous eyes.
I am now free.
we would be the same
if you accepted me heartily (then).
But now I am free.
Yes, I am free . . .
Only I need a good poetic sense
Which can make me happy.

I AM GOING TOWARDS HELL

Good bye dear,
Good bye my love,
Wish you be the same
as i am leaving this fantastic world
and my destiny is to go towards hell
not heaven.

Hell is horrible.
Hell is cruel.
But I am not afraid-
God already has made me strong and straight.

Though I am anxious a little bit,
but god is with me;
and he will help me
and always keep me fit.

so, I am going to hell.
god has sent me an order to stay there
and to make it peaceful and well.
Oh! think—if there is peace in the hell,
Then what will be the shape of the heaven.
it is beyond my words—hell will be the heaven.

BIBHAKAR DUTTA

I DON'T WANT TO EXPECT

What would I expect
in exchange of percept?
fame? a name?
or weeny esteems . . . ??
I am as the same,
know no fame.

Fate though remains
an unfortunate,
I still sense sweetness.
My love and my attachment
never fade
as my Lord always directs.

What would I expect
in exchange?
No glory, no fame
no name, no blame
and nothing is to be left
to become an ashamed.

I know, to expect
means to reject
the real subject
which only remains
and increases our knowledge(s).
It's not yours, and not mine,
It's only my Lord's grace.
I don't expect-only I need that You always bless.

INDIVISIBILITY

Why do you fear, my beloved?
You are charming,
You are excellent,
I am lucky to have you
as my beloved.
But there is a fright,
the fright is to pass you
out of my sight,
the first day of visit
made us for each other,
and, now, I am afraid of
losing you out of my sight.
Yes, I have a fright!,
Everyday is bright
as I still feel your brilliant eyes,
and blithesome smile;
You are my love,
we have to breathe for each other.
Let the world live in its tactful sense,
but we shall build the oneness,
our love will be an instance of indivisibility.
Love seeks sacrifice,
there is no space for incongruity.

BIBHAKAR DUTTA

I'VE GOT A NEW WORD . . .

In my life, I've just got a new word called love,
It's very sweet as well as very hard to have.
I need to be very bold
as everyone says, 'it causes pain, and I should firmly hold '.

It may judge my soul
throwing it into a deep brunt,
yet I am ready to be a hurt.
You know, It's called love!

If it stays still and perfectly,
It will be my fate.
but if it goes away without a certainty,
It will make me worsened and unlucky.

LIFE

No pleasure, no peace,
I like to live in grief.
Life is like the mist-
It cares nothing,
and always makes me a selfish.
Life is so speedy.
It fails to erect my inner sense.
Life is so busy . . .
I am lost,
and I am drowned into senseless emotion.
I almost forget to bestow my passion.
life may be
flowered with love for you or for others,
but this soul is full of insensibility.
So, where is THE LIFE?
Get it to me.
Love!
How many kinds of love we embellish?
Love makes life or life gets love
It's very hard to believe a beloved.
May be sometimes it suitable,
but does life give its solution?
To love and to hurt,
or to hurt after love are the material perception.
An injured soul seeks repletion.
can life give it?
or only consoles to forget it . . . .
An empathetic soul never follows the optimistic speeches.
It always try to find the exact norm.
It needs strength and the great wisdom.

BIBHAKAR DUTTA

But life just knows to hurt.
Life can award only an ungraceful spark!
How many times I beg to my life?
I make imploration
Yet, mind full of frustration.
Are these all illusion?
Illusions for love, for passion, for intimacy . . . . are those sins?
If yes, then I made those hundred times
(mistake)
for love and for my life's shake.
yes, I did such mistake-
yet life could give me a last chance,
though I am not the great sinner;
I could revive my thoughts out of any suspect.

LOVE

Everyday I write new lines,
everyday I write few lines of love;
but words still remains too short
to define the this eternal word.
It's not enough to scribe meaning of love.

Every time I select a new sense,
but it turns into another intent.
Yes, so hard to destine the word,
my hand still seeks the true meaning of love;
my dictionary is still a kid to define the word.

BIBHAKAR DUTTA

LOVE IS FABULOUS

I know, you have a broken heart.
Yes, you have a broken heart!
no one understands your feeling,
but I know, silently you are so much crying.

Today you can't forget your pleasing past,
Alas! your beloved has thrown dust
in your pure love.
Oh, what a disloyalty in today's love!

But a hope still stays in your heart,
it (yet) pardons your beloved.
Love is fabulous,
nobody knows, when we shall have a true match.

Just to wait and wait,
we feel astounded about the past
which once blossomed our love.
So, I still wait for my beloved.

LOVE ME PLEASE . . .

love me please,
I am lost,
I am hurt;
I need a true love.
I am drowned in a dark
kingdom of bad luck.
I need to swim out of there
by your holy love.
My heart has become foul,
I can't tender my love
as it's full of dust.
Only you can make me proud
by your love which is very soft,
pure and bloomed.
Be my love dear-
don't hesitate,
just feel and deem;
I always value your esteem.
You will be my fortune
if you accept my tune.
Love is just like a shadow
if I wait till tomorrow . . .
I need it just
now to meet you on second-life
to finish the sorrow.

BIBHAKAR DUTTA

LOVE VS. ALMIGHTY

There is no place for lament
as your love has refused to be with you.
there is no one to share your feelings
as your love has rejected you.
Now, those days have become wasteful and extravagant.

Each drop shedding from your eyes
wants you to soothe.
But the orphan love always cries.
Now, there is nothing beside you,
to make strong your mood.

So, you should call up your God.
Let Him come inside your soul.
He will redress again your sense,
and you will never be injured (again).
He is the almighty after all.

LUCK

Oh, what a lucky man I am!
the tune emerging from eternity,
would cherish the mankind
assimilating everything-earthy or unearthly.

The song and the meaning
glistering a lover's heart,
light up a way and is forgiving
everything and fulfilling the path.

It's blessed, the voice is God—gifted,
let it expose to bring a motion in everyone's heart;
and the heaven would approach to observe
and bestow our luck that we all eagerly deserve.

MELANCHOLIA

Darkness detects in your face,
have you done anything wrong?
is there anything faulty in your love?
now, you are drowning slowly into a desert.

Look at the sky,
I sometimes surrender my ruthless past,
and feel the blooming, sweet,
and youthful nature.

Please don't allow the overwhelming grief,
don't faint in sorrows,
just a little moment of joy
scrapes such bloomer a lot.

Let the past live in its past,
just allow the ruth to come in your soul.
Say good bye to melancholia,
go and please don't come again you, the past, the harmful
melancholia.

MOTIONLESS

Oh, my love!
this world is not enough
to confer the intensity,
that touches the heart of my beloved.

So much pains . . . !!,
sometimes I fail to sustain,
but you still palp this soul;
my love can't be turned back.

Each day and each night,
end with different accomplishments,
but noiseless, soundless that stays
impatient, is a suffering of this heart.

Without you, the expectation lacks,
without you, the destiny sticks.
being a heedless fellow, I've become a motionless;
only you can shape me an embellished.

BIBHAKAR DUTTA

MY LORD

My Lord has a smiling face
and the world is His trace;
whenever I stand in front of Him
I see His face smiling.

I usually forget what I crave
seeing His charming face;
What would I want . . . ?
He already has bestowed,

and fixed my fate
as every time I confess—He just smiles
and advises me to anticipate-
Oh my Lord is great!!

MY LOVE (PART-2)

My love is like a rose blooming everyday
with a perfect shape
or you may call,
It has got the Fullness.
My love never loses its step,
My love has the depth,
It knows the deepness,
It has got my faith;
My love never fades.
My love knows to convey respect,
It always tends to be exact and perfect.

But my love doesn't allow any tact,
It's very simple in fact.
It doesn't deserve a false praise,
and never tries you to impress.
My love will melt
if your heart bends;
and makes my love its friend.

BIBHAKAR DUTTA

MY LOVE (PART-3)

My love develops day after day,
my love recalls the past,
guides the present,
and dooms the future.
My love grows gradually and day after day.

My love steps slowly and silently,
it just needs your sympathy
to be lengthy.
My love will convey the utmost dignity
if you stay lifelong with me.

My love will show its instance
if our affections become deep and intense,
it will release the illness;
and the barriers of misguidance.
So, please let it come into your sense.

OH DOCTOR

Oh, doctor!!!
Why are you trying to curtail the mankind?
I was suffered from agony;
I was once sunk into the misery.
Now I am cured fully
by your labour and sympathy.
But, you see, doctor-
you are the blessed one
whose proficiency can challenge the mortality.
Hello, doctor!
you are truly a blessed one,
your perceptions are governed by the heaven;
and someone, thus, see this world again.
you are one of my best friends,
and don't estrange it, my dear doctor.
Don't be a professional please,
you are the protector;
we are grateful
as you appease our disease(s).
We know, we are too emotional,
but you are sensitive,
and your hands are very tentative!
Then, why are you trying to curtail the mankind?
Why does you need a bribe??? . . .
We need you very much dear doctor . . .

OH LOVE . . .

Oh love!
let me free from this cruel world-
nothing is pure here,
penurity shrinks my soul,
and absurdity befalls vehemently everywhere.

Today, my journey towards unknown destination,
makes me expectant,
and it's a little bit strange.
Tears shedding down from my eyes,
need to mingle with the waves of sea.

It's too hard to say you—Goodbye!,
but my love—my tears can mingle easily
in this huge deep sea.
Oh, love!!
let me be alone,
and make me free . . . .

I am on the verge of the boat,
the reminiscence of past
lengthens my thrust;
But these waves are enough
to set back the emptiness.
Oh love!! . . .

OH PEACE!

No, I can't see you.
I can feel the absence,
And the absence is dark.
Now, you aren't addressed.
Love calls the souls,
But loses your appearance.
You are blurred.
You now desert.

Heart, mind, soul-
They are out of control.
Where your images reside;
I stay, I follow
And I feel the stillness.
Oh the peace!
Isn't it a poor sacrifice?

Where?? . . .
Where you are, my dear?
No, I need no sign, my dear.
It doesn't become pale.
I will never make it stale.
You may turn,
But I feel peace.

It's hard to appease
The heart made for love.
Oh the peace!
Come and stay by this soul.
Please clam it and wash its foul.
Please come, please come,
Oh peace! . . . .

OUR EYES

Eyes sometimes want to say
if our mind can't dare to say.
Only one word
That makes a pair
of two souls; and
the relationship will be a remarkable,
and they will stay.
So, this is an extraordinary function of our eyes.
Our eyes know
What our heart wants to bestow
and wants to pay.
(to their closest one)
We should respect.
We should not forget.
Our eyes are awesome
as they are God Gifted.

OUR LOVE CAN'T DIE

You are like the glittering spunk
of white sands full of exhilaration
and too proud in love.
You are like the clouds approaching
incessantly to conjugate each other
as to make a shape and to be bigger-
like my love, they are very similar.

Your love can not fail
to store unforgettable moments
as we, like the tides,
can come back soon to seaside.
Love will guide our fate,
and flash out every time
to reflect in our eyes.

Our love can't die,
our love can't be lost;
as the surrender always sustains,
our love will defeat the tort.
Even you go up to the heaven,
and I go towards hell,
our love will still be the same.

PAIN

Pain and pain . . .
Blame and blame . . .
You never want to be a fain?
you capture my veins
blocking the sense
but do stay in core . . .
then—why always you blame?
don't make it vain,
So much pains
I've gathered in my heart;
oh . . . what kind of strain!!
pulling my veins,
You does exist-
I can't retreat,
and, of course, bear our fame.
Oh what a virulent pain!!
You made me cry,
yes, I do try,
I do shed to refresh
my heart with that absolute experience.
Just pain and pain . . . .
I need, I need
do exist with that strain,
but don't blame.
Is It a game??

BIBHAKAR DUTTA

PERFECT

Who says, life is not the best?
life is great,
even much sweeter
than to be a great!
Your love is generous,
It holds your sense
to deploy the honor
and my patience.
So, this life, somehow, has become great.
I am not upset yet-
I need to enlarge my emotion
to fulfill my esteem
and to make you eminent.
So, life is great . . .
My dream was great,
but my love denied
to be a perfect . . .
No, I don't lament,
I don't cry as I am not too sick
to seek my lost love,
Once used to be perfect.
Though my love was not enough,
but my each breath is still comforting-
and it consoles me, says, 'No, it's still perfect.'

PLEASE COME

Please come, stay
and claim your place,
where is the sense love with out you??
Oh! your absence becomes so painful
but our love must be true.
I wish, I could stain each word
in the name of my beloved;
please come, stay . . .
and give me a clue;
The story is merely vague without you.
Let's bind a bond
that could belaud our love to be true.

RAINY SEASON

The rain spreading its hands
to enwrap the river
are shedding rainy shower.
The river seems frenzy
blended by rainy water.

Clouds, lightning and spark,
look so exhilarated
for their visit to earth.
I am standing at the bank of river
searching for the holy water
to make my soul consecrate by heavenly shower.

It's truly great-
you are, the rainy season,
just emanate your holy shower
to create a soothing joy like the heaven.
Yes, you are great, rainy season . . .

REWARD

I want a reward,
A reward that makes me feel
every day and night,
I want an award that will help me to overstay this life (only
for you).

I want to have your sweet senses
those would stay in this earth overlong.
This reward of rewards is nothing but your love-
oh! just be my beloved.

You will be my praise and all
if the affinity continues lifelong;
a visit is enough and will make worthy my effort,
just feel the strength-the firmness of love, but don't distort.

The reward that can spell the chapter of love,
and explain the heartiness of beloved.
There is no call for an equipotential challenge,
just be my beloved, oh . . !! my beloved . . .

BIBHAKAR DUTTA

SHAPE

Everyday my love gets a shape,
it's pure and, of course, faultless,
each day ends with an expect
but might be confused!

she feels lack, betrayed
and fails to expect.
No, love will emanate,
the soul can't deny;

and you shouldn't defy,
just look at me-
it's gleaming into our eyes
and trying to give a shape.

SHED OF DIVINITY

Wise, greatness have their way(s),
As I am here, I must pay
world's gratefulness.
Oh god!
Help me to depart from this tough surface-
I need hide in the shed of divinity.
No fury, no fury-
Just restful moments will play
in my heart to fulfill my story.
but I must pay, believe me.
I need pass through this way
where I want my Lord to stay
with me.
No false pride, no glory-
I just want my Lord to stay
beside me.
Yes, I need His grace;
My fate is waiting to be blessed
Staying under divine shed.
Wise, pride, glory have their own way(s).

BIBHAKAR DUTTA

SPRING'S SHED

My heart gets a shake,
oh, my love comes back!!
and wants to spread,
under spring's shed.
To get back the earlier sense,
I need to be mingled with its fragrance,
yes, the fragrance!! . . .
by that, I shall have its influence,
and my love will stand sharply
in front of eyes of my mistress,
but not a further pretense.
Standing at the edge of city street,
I am to perceive her sweet percept;
still splendid is her face!
let it grow under spring's shed.

STILLNESS

Stillness and love-
I think, they are friends,
love improves in silence;
love is deepened in stillness.

The room is now silent,
and my heart is friendless;
my love for my beloved
gradually emanates.

So, I give you my consent-
It's very pleasant
to feel you in such sense,
I will allow no one instead of my loneliness.

BIBHAKAR DUTTA

STRAIGHT

I am happy
because I like to stain my each vain
with Tragedy.
I need pains.
More pains
mean more achievements . . . .
But I have to stand straight.
God is watching me.
He will give me a gift
if I pass through this tragic street (of life).
So, I have to stand straight.
Yes, straight . . . .

TENDING TOWARDS ETERNITY

My heart, my soul
my sorrows, my luck
stay in a state of deep faith,
It will not leave me
as every time I breath
under a true sense of divinity.
If my fate betrays me, however,
I am so excited and eager
to cultivate the sweetness sense of infinity.
(The part of divinity)
Nowadays, my soul is going to uplift
towards a stage or you may call it-
'tending towards eternity'.

THE BED

He is lying like a dead
on his bed,
the bed is mossy, flowery and greeny
where he contemplates his past,
and looks for eternity.
He didn't forget his lost love yet,
he was snatched by a false emotion.
He is lying like a dead
without any notion,
just the bed is his true mate
which leads his soul into motion.
The bed is long stretched,
and the blue sky is smiling above his head.
The bed is his true mate . . .

THE BEGGAR

I am not a beggar
as you think.
I have no thrust
for your love.
I do not want to flatter (you).
I have no intention to bluff.

In these days, I have learnt to scatter
the poesy style to sound better.
So, I pray to you, my God-
it's your wish
that I've got
to adorn my poetic plot.
I am a beggar.
Oh! my God.
Yes, I am . . .
I want to attach with the heavenly thoughts,
and I know a rich
can never reach
in the area of eminence
that only you holds;
and maintains its progress.
Please my God help me.
Help this beggar . . . .

THE CROWN

Where dynasty follows welfare,
the people gather
and bestow there ultimate sensibility;
and the crown feels mercy
addressing his followers:
'This is my democracy-
God is merciful towards my kingdom,
I've been allowed
to bring up His desire
by accelerating the power of a good democracy.'
The crown stands for humanity and for the commonwealth,
there is no place to adorn false pride;
he knows, his Lord is against of vanity.
People, hither, pray for their master's breath,
but never pay a debt.
Everyone says, 'Our king is perfect,
oh, what a great state!,
what a blessed dynasty! . . .'.
At the time of events, they pertain its gains,
and gather when the celebration
comes to be a perfect.
Oh, what a beautiful state!
They inquire of their king's wit
as the king wants to attach the kinship,
people never forget to offer their cakes-
the king, they expect, is a God-gifted.
What a blissful state!!

They will raise their hands
declaring their fate,
for the crown's sake.
They have got a prestige-
after all, their king is a true humanist-
oh! what a wonderful state . . . !

THE DAY OF DELIGHT

Today is conjunction of two seasons,
winter likely wants to enter
in the state of autumn.
I am walking in the street
and sensing the presence of winter.

Faded field, dry wind
just make the day mopish a little bit,
but there is an quiescence in air
which stirs my mind,
and the afternoon is bright.

An unknown and strange sense
I can guess,
changing of feeling and a restive emotion
want to assimilate before Its arrival.
Today is the day of delight.

THE DAY OF DELIGHT (PART-2)

This is my life,
and I am watching the sky
sitting on in this earth
beside a lake,
with a vacant mood;
I think it's the best time
to feel the blessedness of this earth.
A busy one can't have sense
of importance of this moment,
and will not acquire the completeness
ignoring such fantastical sight.
Big lake, bright light,
layers of pearly water,
everything is bloomed and bright.
Oh God,
what a charming day of delight!
Don't miss the day,
come, don't be a moody and sit by me,
and let's enjoy the day of delight.
Dear friends, come,
don't delay;
leave your busy day.

THE END

A day follows another day,
and that reaches closer to destiny,
is only death.
The death is our final destiny,
are you ready to face?

Salvation waits after this horrific end,
death makes a history;
It's an extreme fact-
life ends its search.
Death is priceless,
It's the end.

THE KITES

There was nothing
for what I would mourn,
those days were excellent-
not like now.
I didn't know,
where I was going . . . .
just ran after the kites;
sometimes I stopped,
and chased even faster than before,
but the kites seemed to be away,
didn't want to stay for the world
of sorrow.
They are free, out of gloom,
just like my childhood days;
today, everything is shapeless;
I'm delighted staying with my earlier remembrance,
those days were really amazing!!
now, I am missing.

BIBHAKAR DUTTA

THE LONELINESS

This loneliness is a gift for me,
the stillness enhances my emotion,
my heart is staved;
yet your affection compensates my all folly.

The loneliness strikes my heart very much,
but our attachment spreads over this tort
calming my soul, and I get everyday a new step,
my love is like a fulgent bright light.

Loneliness gives me a pain every time,
and I am always ready to face and clasp.
I know it just gives me shock,
but my love is untamed and undefeated,
thereby I will love you much and much . . .
Oh, my beloved!!!

THE ROOM

Let the wind come in the room to clean up trashes.
Full of delusion, out of freshness,
Lack of frenzy
Dismiss the room.
Soothing air should fill up its emptiness
And remove the dullness.

Like the way,
My heart and my soul
Should be freshened up by my self-control.
Let the love come, and go in my heart
To clam my sense
And to save it become a desert.

They both are my part.
The room is the little hut
Full of my curious sense(s) and cognizance.
Love restores my heart,
And reclaims my mind
To become a desert.

THE WAY OF MY LIFE

The way of my earlier life
Left behind my past,
Was enough
To confer my love.
My love is now haggish,
And I am an ungracious.

Pride, emotion, affection
Are formless without very perfection.
To mold my love again
May become shameful and vain.
Time is indomitable,
But I've been given;
I've been dignified with so many opportunities.
I am just a failure to control my fate, my love, and its
necessities.

I just want to express
my regard to you, oh! beloved-
I need to extend the time
to solve the repugnance
chapter of this life.
Believe me, end will become blissful and destroy the grief.

TO LOVE

Past was mournful,
out of delight,
lack of jollity,
my mind was feeling an absence
and was almost blank.

Now, a new moment,
fresh sense,
exciting experiences
are fulfilling the want;
and my heart is waiting for second love.

All will be lost,
your dearest one may refuse the promises,
but love remains the same.
It doesn't have any past
as love only knows much to love.

TO MOAN

To stick into your eyes
means to get my love back-
Well, I glance it,
But I lost that at once.
Why??
Sometimes I ask myself.
Love should be perceived through its real essence
And longed by a deepest heart
Which I used to feel once.

Now, I realize, why didn't it extend in my life?
I shadowed you behind
my pride.
I failed to adjudge our love.
We couldn't become same
And two didn't change into the ONE . . .
To moan and only the spleenful songs have to be sung
Sitting beside my love.

TOMORROW

Who knows the tomorrow?
may be fair, out of fear,
Vision would be perfect and clear.
We could expect our dears closer-
Consciousness may rule to dissolve our sorrow(s).
so, who knows the tomorrow??

But please, don't come disaster
to ruin our future,
to destroy our dreams,
and don't come to sink us in fear.
Please go back to hell
as the tomorrow will sit beside the heaven.

BIBHAKAR DUTTA

TRAGIC MELODY

What can I do?
nothing, just to surrender
myself to my love as
I am a helpless before the tragic melody.
Oh! it's too strong,
and absorbs gloominess by its intensity.
Oh! the tragic melody . . .

Love, dejection, faithlessness
I know all these trifle
inside a broken heart;
but we also have a lesson,
please listen
the melody immersing from an inamorato heart.
Oh! tragic melody . . .

TRUTH

The truth is waiting behind you,
love was only the hope;
but you have thrown it on sty.
Now, I think, how can I heal?
I am your beloved, not a spy.
The truth was once our life,
the truth was our pride,
but today It is a sentiment
as for our detachment.
I don't know, who is right,
or what makes it wrong?
The truth tells about our love,
and I get something more than worldly covenant.
The past has passed
though my love still lives in stillness;
our love exceeds the bond,
that's why, I will love you forever.
Now, I am so much proud
as I am to make my love eternal,
exceeding bouts.

BIBHAKAR DUTTA

WAVES

Waves and waves,
Oh, what a sparkling view!
I notice right here standing at the sea beach;
we all are excited,
we are spirited
playing with waves
forgetting the tomorrow.
who knows the tomorrow?? . . .
That forbids hopes,
and invites uncertainty,
we should not follow-
the beach is now bright,
immortalize each second
leaving worries of tomorrow.
It's a moment to blend
with this beauteous earth,
please don't invite tomorrow
as a friend of sorrow.

WILL MY LOVE MAKE ME FREE?

Will my love make me free?
Does it strike me mentally?
Does it maintain ideality?
A true love does it . . .

So, my dear please hurt me;
just give me pain,
and I will be perfect again and again.
Just give me the pain . . .

Yes, my soul will get strain,
and my blood will pull the pain.
(again and again)
So, my dear love me
and do hurt me . . .

If your love makes me pure,
I will be someday free.
But you should always be in glee
as you love me, and I am very much sure.

WINTER

The day is beautiful,
windy and parky,
winter has arrived;
stillness starts to absorb our mind.

Soul becomes frisky,
and full of thoughts,
it's very mellifluous
to sit by warmth.

Winter gives the chance
to flourish our reflection
musing all the day,
and for a sweet inception.

WINTER AFTERNOON

Standing at the mid of city street,
I bethought myself as a king of my own kingdom
forgetting sorrows of daily life.
I was lost in an another world
standing by the footpath,
you may call it a harborage of mobs,
or a busy park.

Now, I took a step towards my home,
but I enjoyed the walk perceiving
a different mood in that warm winter afternoon.
So, I say, 'You may have tried many times your luck,
sometimes you've got a lot, or sometimes you lose,
but do pass a moment that refreshes your breath,
and makes you a smart'.

BIBHAKAR DUTTA

WOUNDS

Wounds fulfill to expect me (again)
that memory of love dethroned by misfortune.
Though I do not lament every time,
but sometimes it's too hard
to console this heart.
I spent, I enjoyed,
and I was overjoyed
by the sweetness of love.
I smiled as love is blind,
now I fail to define—who I am?
Now my love says, 'I am lost'.
My heart says, 'You are of no cost'.
Alas! no way to leave my past,
Sometimes it glitters,
Sometimes it allows me to suffer.

YOUR LOVE IS ENOUGH . . .

Your love is perfect, full of incitement
and insets a perpetual affection.
Though it stayed for a while,
but it's enough to feel your sincerity.
I have got that attachment
by my heart,
and I already told you,
This is enough for me
to place it in my heart permanently.
In this busy world,
everything takes a new shape continuously,
Yet, your sweet face sweetens
my soul ceaselessly.
I am still of little sense,
but sparing to conserve my past,
I doesn't want to tautologize;
yes, your love is enough . . . .
Oh my beloved!!!

BIBHAKAR DUTTA

www.ingramcontent.com/pod-product-compliance
Lightning Source LLC
Chambersburg PA
CBHW071245170526
45165CB00003B/1240